EVIDENCE OF THINGS UNSEEN

An Introduction to Fundamental Theology

WORKBOOK

EVIDENCE OF THINGS UNSEEN

An Introduction to Fundamental Theology

WORKBOOK

TAN Books
Gastonia, North Carolina

Compiled by Melissa Girard

Robert Klesko, contributing author

Cover image: *Disputation of the Holy Sacrament*, Raphael (1483–1520)

Series design by Margaret Ryland

Cover and layout by Caroline Green

ISBN: 978-1-5051-1935-0

Published in the United States by
TAN Books
PO Box 269
Gastonia, NC 28053
www.TANBooks.com

Printed in India

Contents

A Note to Instructors vii

PART I: HOW DO WE KNOW ABOUT GOD?
Chapter 1: The Desire for God 1
Chapter 2: Natural Revelation 5
Chapter 3: Divine Revelation 9

PART II: WHAT IS SACRED SCRIPTURE?
Chapter 1: Divine Inspiration 15
Chapter 2: How Was the Bible Put Together? 19
Chapter 3: Sacred Scripture in the Life of the Church 23

PART III: INTERPRETING SCRIPTURE
Chapter 1: Authentic Interpretation of Scripture 29
Chapter 2: Criteria for Interpreting Scripture 33
Chapter 3: The Bible in Relation to Science and History 37

PART IV: OVERVIEW OF THE BIBLE
Chapter 1: The Old Testament 43
Chapter 2: The New Testament 47
Chapter 3: The Unity of the Old and New Testaments 51

PART V: THE GOSPELS
Chapter 1: The Gospels' Central Place in Scripture 57
Chapter 2: The Synoptic Gospels: Matthew, Mark, and Luke 61
Chapter 3: The Gospel of John 65

Final Exam 68

Answer Key 71

A Note to Instructors

As Pope St. John Paul II made clear in his apostolic exhortation *Catechesi Tradendae*, "the definitive aim of catechesis is to put people not only in touch but in communion, in intimacy, with Jesus Christ." The *Formed in Christ* series seeks to fulfill this call, fostering intimacy with Christ through its dynamic content.

Rather than presenting religion as any other subject to be mastered, our series editors have designed each text to plumb the bottomless genius of Catholicism found in centuries of theologians, saints, councils, and papal teachings.

The six volumes in *Formed in Christ* cover every point in the USCCB's guidelines for high school catechesis.

In *Evidence of Things Unseen*, the course of study will survey God's revelation of himself in Scripture and Tradition. It details what revelation is and how it came about in history, including how the Bible was put together. The book gives an overview of Scripture, focusing especially on the Gospels and their prominence in the life of the Church.

This supplemental workbook is designed to provide instructors with test material and direction for enhancing students' grasp of the material.

For each chapter, the following components are included:

Memory Verse

Appealing not only to the head but also the heart, a suitable memory verse, chosen for its relation to the chapter's content, is suggested to help the student with their prayer life. Throughout the week, have your student attempt to recite this verse from memory.

Key Terms

A list of key terms from the chapter is included. Students are encouraged to write down some notes about these terms (either here in the workbook or in a separate notebook) using not only the text but the *Catechism of the Catholic Church* and a good Catholic dictionary as well. This will not only prepare students for testing but deepen their understanding of the content.

Questions for Review

Taken directly from the student text, the Questions for Review, provided in "short answer" format, ensure comprehension of the material. Answers are provided in the back.

Quiz

For each chapter, ten questions are provided for testing. Multiple Choice, True or False, and Fill-in-the-Blank quizzes vary throughout the workbook. Answers are provided in the back.

Questions for Discussion

Dialogue between students and instructors is essential. Not only will the Questions for Discussion (included both here and in the student text) provide another opportunity for reinforcing the material but the questions are specifically designed to prompt students to reflect on their own faith experience. While discussion between students and instructors is highly recommended, the Questions for Discussion can also be used as prompts for personal writing exercises. Since these are more for personal reflection, no answers are provided.

Essay Topics and/or Further Study

The *Formed in Christ* series is designed to expose students to Church documents and the writings of theologians from all stages of Church history. But these selected readings are just the beginning of Catholic thought that students can discover. The Essay Topics and/or Further Study suggestions encourage students to dig deeper into the wealth of Catholic teaching through independent study. A mix of personal, subjective prompts and research topics, these suggestions will enable your student to learn more about their Catholic faith. Grading is left up to the instructor's discretion.

Final Exam

In the back, you will find a final exam that aggregates all the most important content. This provides a barometer for how well your student(s) absorbed the material. It consists of matching and short answer. Answers are provided in the back.

Part I

How Do We Know about God?

Part I: Chapter 1

The Desire for God

Memory Verse

> God created man in his own image, in the image of God he created him; male and female he created them. And God blessed them, and God said to them, "Be fruitful and multiply, and fill the earth and subdue it; and have dominion over the fish of the sea and over the birds of the air and over every living thing that moves upon the earth."
>
> —Genesis 1:27–28

Key Terms

Happiness

Anthropology

Creation

Nature

Paradise

The Fall

Natural Revelation

Divine Revelation

Questions for Review

1. What does "anthropology" mean?

2. What does it mean to be created in God's image?

3. What is the "Fall"?

4. When man and woman sinned, what did they lose?

5. What problems have we inherited from our first parents?

Quiz

1. The key to happiness is:
   A. peace and security.
   B. communion with God.
   C. reaching one's goals.

2. True or False: In addition to humans, animals are created in God's image.
   True
   False

3. Adam and Eve were created by God:
   A. in a state of holiness.
   B. so that they were not solitary.
   C. both a and b.

4. Original Sin:
   A. is passed on to all humans.
   B. only affects Christians.
   C. can be overcome through our own power and will.

5. Natural Revelation is how:
   A. God speaks to his people.
   B. God reveals himself through creation.
   C. God uses his power throughout the cosmos.

6. Divine Revelation is how:
   A. humanity interprets mystical signs.
   B. creation makes God's plan clear.
   C. God reveals himself directly to humanity.

7. Mankind can discover important truths about God and his nature through:
   A. their feelings.
   B. revelation alone.
   C. the use of reason.

8. The Incarnation describes:
   A. the creation of the natural world.
   B. when Jesus Christ became man.
   C. when the soul uses the power of reason.

9. Total happiness and peace are found:
   A. in the absence of war.
   B. when we are in a state of grace.
   C. in heaven alone.

10. *Gaudium et Spes* says that, "Only in ________________ can man direct himself toward goodness."
   A. freedom
   B. service
   C. faith

Questions for Discussion

1. Have you ever wanted something very badly and then been disappointed when you finally got it or discovered it wasn't enough? Describe what happened.
2. What are things you want most in life? Do they have anything in common?
3. Where and when do you find the most peace?

Essay Topics and/or Further Study

1. God created men and women in his image. How do you think this shapes Catholic teaching on the human person?
2. St. Augustine taught that "our hearts are restless until they rest" in God. In what ways do you see restlessness in the world around you? How can people find true peace?
3. What are some ways you believe God reveals himself in created nature? Can you think of an example of something in nature that has taught you about who God is?
4. God reveals himself directly to man through Divine Revelation. What are some examples from Scripture when God spoke directly to his people? Choose one example and describe how you would feel if you were present.
5. Reflect on the selected reading from *Gaudium et Spes*. Choose one paragraph and discuss how you think it is relevant to issues or occurrences you experience in your own life.

Part I: Chapter 2

Natural Revelation

Memory Verse

> For from the greatness and beauty of created things comes a corresponding perception of their Creator.
>
> —Wisdom 13:5

Key Terms

Natural Revelation

Fathers of the Church

St. Thomas Aquinas

Scholasticism

The Five Ways of Knowing God

First Vatican Council

Skepticism

Relativism

Soul

Questions for Review

1. What is Natural Revelation?

2. What is looking at God's creation supposed to lead us to do?

3. Can we know that God exists by reason alone?

4. Name and explain each of St. Thomas Aquinas's five ways for knowing God from Natural Revelation.

5. What is relativism? How does it undermine reason?

Quiz

1. God is knowable through our experience of __________.

2. The movement to integrate philosophical method and Christianity to describe and explain revealed truth was called __________.

3. St. Thomas's proof of God's existence from the argument of Motion states, "Whatever is in motion is __________."

4. God is the first, or uncaused ________.

5. The argument from ______________ holds that God is the standard of all goodness, perfection, and truth.

6. It is reasonable to conclude that a ____________________ is the author of all that exists.

7. The First Vatican Council responded to the skeptical philosophies that emerged from ______________.

8. ______________ claims that truth does not exist.

9. The Catechism explains that the ________ can "have its origin only in God."

10. Our desire for truth, goodness, and happiness are aspects of our desire ___________________.

Questions for Discussion

1. Have you ever stood on a beach or a mountaintop or looked at the stars and felt close to God? If so, why do you think this is?
2. What evidence of God do you see in nature?
3. Why do you tell others about yourself? Why do you think God would want to tell us about himself? Why would he want us to know him?

Essay Topics and/or Further Study

1. Reflect on St. Francis's "Canticle of the Sun." Choose three aspects of Creation that reveal something specific about God to humanity.
2. Do you think it is possible for a person to come to believe in God by witnessing nature? What Scripture or testimony of the Church Fathers support your position?
3. Construct a two-sided dialogue with an atheist. Choose one of St. Thomas Aquinas's proofs for the existence of God and write up a hypothetical conversation.
4. The Church has emphasized time and again why the use of reason is so important. How do you exercise reason? What happens when the use of reason is abandoned? Think of one concrete example to illustrate your point.
5. Pope Benedict quotes Psalm 8:3–4, which says, "When I look at your heavens, the work of your fingers, the moon and the stars which you have established; what is man that you are mindful of him, and the son of man that you care for him?" Why do you think God created the vast world and yet "the summit of all creation" is, Pope Benedict says, "man and woman"?

Part 1: Chapter 3

Divine Revelation

Memory Verse

> The fear of the LORD is the beginning of wisdom.
>
> —PROVERBS 9:10

(or)

> But when the time had fully come, God sent forth his Son, born of woman, born under the law, to redeem those who were under the law, so that we might receive adoption as sons. And because you are sons, God has sent the Spirit of his Son into our hearts, crying, "Abba! Father!" So through God you are no longer a slave but a son, and if a son then an heir.
>
> —GALATIANS 4:4–7

Key Terms

Divine Revelation

Patriarchs

Israelites

Wisdom Literature

Prophets

The Deposit of Faith

Sacred Tradition

Magisterium

Sensus fidei

The Apostolate

Questions for Review

1. Who are the Patriarchs? What is their relationship to one another and to God?

2. Through whom did God give the Law to Israel, and under whom did God establish Israel as a great kingdom?

3. Which prophet bridged the gap between the Old Testament and the New?

4. Who is the summation of the Scriptures and why?

5. In what two ways is Divine Revelation transmitted to each new generation? Define each way.

Quiz

True/False

1. ____ Abraham means "the father of a multitude of nations."
2. ____ The new law God gave to the Israelites after they broke their covenant with him is outlined in the book of Exodus.
3. ____ After the time of David, his kingdom was divided into the Kingdom of Israel and the Kingdom of Judah.
4. ____ The Old Testament Wisdom Literature includes the books of Job, Proverbs, and Numbers, among others.
5. ____ John the Baptist can be called an Old Testament Prophet even though his story is in the New Testament.
6. ____ The full message of Divine Revelation is called the Deposit of Truth.
7. ____ Scripture and Tradition both come from the preaching of the apostles.
8. ____ The office of authoritative interpretation and teaching of the Deposit of Faith is called Mystagogy.
9. ____ The laity's responsibility is to influence the wider culture only through their prayer life.
10. ____ The apostolate calls the laity to pursue lives of holiness and bring the faith to the culture at large.

Questions for Discussion

1. What does the way God slowly revealed himself in history tell us about him? Why do you think he chose to reveal himself in this way?
2. How does God's "education" of Israel remind you of your own education?
3. How much of a priority is it for you to read and study what God has communicated about himself? Should it be more of a priority in your life? Why or why not?

Essay Topics and/or Further Study

1. Choose one of the Patriarchs to study further. Find their story in Scripture and retell the main events of their life. What was their relationship with God like? What message did they share with the people of Israel? What can you learn from their example in your own life?
2. Read the *Catechism* paragraph 64 (on page 31 in the text). With the help of Scripture, compare three of the holy women listed to the Blessed Mother.
3. Write a letter to a non-Catholic (you can make one up if you do not want to compose a real letter) explaining not only what the Deposit of Faith is but how it is transmitted. How is the faith that you practice today connected to the past?
4. The laity are called to bring faith to the world by participating directly in our culture's social, economic, and political life while pursuing lives of holiness. Share an example of someone you believe lives the apostolate well. How do they bring Jesus into the world?
5. The Catholic Church believes that Jesus Christ is the "summation" of all the Scriptures. Reflect on what you have learned about who Jesus is directly from the Bible. Cite both Old and New Testament passages.

Part II

What Is Sacred Scripture?

Part II: Chapter 1

Divine Inspiration

Memory Verse

> All scripture is inspired by God and profitable for teaching, for reproof, for correction, and for training in righteousness.
>
> —2 Timothy 3:16

Key Terms

Divine Inspiration

Theopneustos

Historical context

Literary context

Literal interpretation

Inerrancy

Questions for Review

1. Who inspired the Sacred Scriptures?

2. What does it mean to take historical context into account when studying the Scriptures?

3. What does it mean to take literary context into account when studying the Scriptures?

4. What is inerrancy?

5. Is everything in the Bible "literally" true? Explain.

Quiz

1. The Sacred Scriptures were written by ________________ through the inspiration of ________________________.

2. God used the "powers and abilities" of human authors and also gave them the gift of ________________________ to write Sacred Scripture.

3. The Greek word *theopneustos* means ________________.

4. ________________ is both sacred and true.

5. Taking into account the time and place in which the Scriptures were written provides the reader with ____________________________.

6. By reading Scripture within its proper ________________, we are able to understand more fully the authors' ________________.

7. ____________________________ takes into consideration the genre or type of text we read.

8. To describe a writing as ____________________ is to proclaim that it is free from all ____________.

9. Even Doctors of the Church, such as ____________________________, had difficulty understanding what they thought seemed to be inconsistencies or errors in Scripture.

10 The interpretation of Sacred Scripture is guided by the Church's ________________.

Questions for Discussion

1. Both Jesus and the Scriptures are referred to as "the Word of God." What does this tell you about how we should treat the Scriptures?
2. Can you think of a situation in which knowing someone's history or background has helped you understand their words or actions better? If so, describe it. What does this tell you about the role of context in studying the Scriptures?
3. What do you think makes the Bible more credible than any other book? Explain.

Essay Topics and/or Further Study

1. Considering the meaning of inerrancy: Are there any passages in Scripture that you find difficult to accept as "free from error"? Where can you go to learn more about what the Church teaches on that issue?
2. Choose a passage from Scripture and investigate its historical background. How does more information about the history, politics, or culture of the people and places in this passage help you better understand its meaning?
3. Pope Benedict XVI wrote that "belief in the biblical narrative is as necessary to salvation as is belief in the doctrines of the faith." How would your life change if you decided to reject the Bible's inerrancy?
4. The supplemental reading by Leon J. Suprenant explains the distinction between the *literal* sense of Scripture and a *literalistic* interpretation. Define what these terms mean and explain why this can lead readers to make different conclusions about Scripture.
5. List and explain all of the attributes you think are necessary for a biblical scholar. What kinds of knowledge, skills, and personal traits do you think would better help a biblical scholar to understand Scripture?

Part II: Chapter 2

How Was the Bible Put Together?

Memory Verse

> Go therefore and make disciples of all nations, baptizing them in the name of the Father and of the Son and of the Holy Spirit, teaching them to observe all that I have commanded you.

—Matthew 28:19–20

Key Terms

Canon of Scripture

Oral Tradition

Ecumenical Council

Synod

Gnosticism

Apocryphal

Dynamic equivalency

Questions for Review

1. What is Oral Tradition?

2. What do we mean by the phrase "the canon of Scripture"?

3. For the early Church, what was the ultimate criteria for a book being granted canonical status?

4. By what century did the bishops first give us the canon of Scripture that the Church still uses today?

6. What is dynamic equivalency?

Quiz

1. The books of the New Testament were written:
   A. in the first century after the death of Jesus.
   B. beginning with St. Paul until the Council of Nicaea.
   C. from the time of the apostles until the Middle Ages.

2. The apostles spread the Gospel through preaching, in what is referred to as:
   A. ministry.
   B. oral tradition.
   C. Pentecost.

3. Early magisterial statements concerning the canon of Scripture were made to clarify:
   A. theological questions.
   B. who the authors of Scripture were.
   C. which books could be used in the Liturgy.

4. The first person to use the word "canon" to refer to the list of New Testament books was:
   A. St. Athanasius.
   B. St. Jerome.
   C. St. Augustine.

5. The list of inspired books that make up our Scripture today was first promulgated at:
   A. the Synod of Rome in 382.
   B. the Council of Hippo in 393.
   C. the Council at Carthage in 397.

6. Gnosticism denies:
   A. the inerrancy of Scripture.
   B. the authority of the apostles.
   C. the true humanity of Christ.

7. The early Church held that for a book to be granted canonical status, it needed three characteristics: apostolic origin, universal acceptance, and:
   A. papal approval.
   B. liturgical use.
   C. confirmed authorship.

8. Apocryphal means:
   A. "not authentic."
   B. "the end times."
   C. "accepted translated."

9. The New Testament was first written in:
   A. Latin.
   B. Aramaic.
   C. Greek.

10. Dynamic equivalency seeks to preserve a text's:
    A. exact words.
    B. original meaning.
    C. historical context.

Questions for Discussion

1. Why is it important that the New Testament books were written by eyewitnesses of Jesus's ministry or close companions of eyewitnesses? What do we gain from this?
2. The Scripture you hear at Mass is the same Scripture Christians have heard for nearly two thousand years. What does this teach us about the power of God's Word to speak to us in our own time and place?
3. Why is it important to have both the written Word of God and the preaching of the priests and bishops? What do we gain by having both?

Essay Topics and/or Further Study

1. Write an encyclopedia entry on the topic of the canon of Scripture. Define the canon and recap all the significant historical events related to it.
2. Choose a New Testament writing by one of the apostles or their companions. Study it well, then set aside your Bible. In your own words, share the message of the Scripture. Now refer back to the Bible. How does your presentation differ?
3. What are the three characteristics the early Church believed the canonical books of the New Testament shared? Explain each of the three traits and why you believe they were relevant.
4. Hundreds of English translations of the Bible exist. Find three different translations of the same verse (you can do this online). What is different about the translations? Do you see an advantage to certain translations? Why do you think certain translations can be problematic?
5. If you were asked by a Protestant how their Bible is different from your Catholic Bible, how would you respond? Explain the apocryphal books. Referencing St. Athanasius's "Festal Letter 39" (pages 67–69 in the text), show why these books are part of the Church's canon of Scripture.

Part II: Chapter 3

Sacred Scripture in the Life of the Church

Memory Verse

> Your Word is a lamp for my feet and a light for my path.
>
> —Psalm 119:105

Key Terms

Theology

The Liturgy of the Hours

The Divine Office

Liturgy of the Word

Ambo

Lectionary

Lectio Divina

Rosary

Questions for Review

1. What is theology?

2. What is another name for the Liturgy of the Hours? What is the role of Scripture in this prayer?

3. Name three prayers in the Mass that are drawn from Sacred Scripture.

4. What is *lectio divina*?

5. How does the Rosary incorporate Scripture into personal prayer?

Quiz

True/False

1. ____ Vatican II calls Scripture "the soul of sacred theology."
2. ____ The Liturgy of the Hours is made up of ten "hours," or periods of prayer.
3. ____ The Liturgy of the Hours has its roots in Greek temple worship.
4. ____ Scripture readings at Mass are read from a lectern or pulpit called a lectionary.
5. ____ The readings for Mass have been chosen for their connection to the liturgical day.
6. ____ The most appropriate home for Sacred Scripture is in the Liturgy of the Hours.
7. ____ A prayerful method of reading Scripture is called *lectio divina.*

8. ____ The Our Father and Hail Mary are biblical prayers.

9. ____ All twenty mysteries of the Rosary are directly recorded in Scripture.

10 ____ The Rosary is a contemplative prayer.

Questions for Discussion

1 Have you ever heard people say that Catholics don't believe in studying the Bible? Why do you think they say this?

2. Have you ever read or heard a passage from the Bible that spoke to your heart in a very direct way? Describe what happened. Why do you think the Bible can do this?

3. To what extent do you incorporate the Bible into your personal prayer life? What else could you do to spend more time with God's word?

Essay Topics and/or Further Study

1. Discuss the role of Scripture in theology. How does the Church understand Scripture's significance to theology? What should a theologian's relationship with Scripture entail?

2. Find the prayers of the Liturgy of the Hours in a breviary or online. Try praying all the hours in one day. Reflect on your experience. What impact did the prayers and readings have on your day? Will you continue this practice?

3. Research the prayers of the Mass to find just how much Scripture is used in the Liturgy. Whole books have been written on this topic! Summarize where Scripture is used in each part of the Mass. With this information, how "biblical" do you think the Mass is? Does this change the way you see the Liturgy?

4. Choose a passage from the Gospels to practice *lectio divina*. After you go through all four steps of the process, write out your reflections for each of the four. What are the advantages of praying with *lectio divina*? How does it differ from how you normally read Scripture?

5. There are four sets of mysteries of the Rosary. Choose one set and research the Scripture passages behind each individual mystery.

Part III

Interpreting Scripture

Part III: Chapter 1

Authentic Interpretation of Scripture

Memory Verse

> When the Spirit of truth comes, he will guide you into all the truth; for he will not speak on his own authority, but whatever he hears he will speak, and he will declare to you the things that are to come.
>
> —John 16:13

Key Terms

Exegesis

Historical critical method

Divino Afflante Spiritu

Dei Verbum

Interpretation of the Bible in the Church

Questions for Review

1. What is exegesis?

2. What are the goals of the historical-critical method?

3. How did *Divino Afflante Spiritu* affect biblical scholarship?

4. What was the Second Vatican Council's document on Sacred Scripture called?

5. What is a common theme of all the modern Church documents on Scripture?

Quiz

1. Jesus gave the authority and responsibility to interpret Scripture properly to:
   A. the Church Fathers.
   B. the apostles and their successors.
   C. the Pharisees and Sadducees.

2. The task of interpreting Scripture is called:
   A. exposition.
   B. explication.
   C. exegesis.

3. Christians need ____________________ to understand what Scripture means.
   A. historical evidence
   B. Church tradition
   C. degrees in theology

4. The form of research used to study Scripture in the eighteenth and nineteenth centuries was called:
   A. source criticism.
   B. the original biblical languages method.
   C. the historical-critical method.

5. The new form of research used to aid Scripture study sought to:
   A. better understand the people and events in Scripture through facts.
   B. put the books of Scripture into chronological order based on carbon dating.
   C. prove which writings were or were not considered sacred.

6. The document ________________________ provides the basis for the Catholic understanding of Revelation and Scripture.
   A. *Divino Afflante Spiritu*
   B. *Dei Verbum*
   C. *Interpretation of Scripture*

7. The document ___________________________ gives detail on interpretive methods used by Catholic Bible scholars.
   A. *Divino Afflante Spiritu*
   B. *Dei Verbum*
   C. *Interpretation of Scripture*

8. The document _____________________ opened the door for the use of modern methods of biblical interpretation and encouraged the use of the original languages in Scriptures (Hebrew and Greek) for study and translation.
   A. *Divino Afflante Spiritu*
   B. *Dei Verbum*
   C. *Interpretation of Scripture*

9. The document _______________________ encouraged the use of Hebrew and Greek in Scripture study.
   A. *Divino Afflante Spiritu*
   B. *Dei Verbum*
   C. *Interpretation of Scripture*

10. All modern Church documents on Scripture emphasize the need for:
    A. advanced degrees in theology.
    B. all Catholics to study Scripture.
    C. more Scripture in the Liturgy.

Questions for Discussion

1. Do you think scholars should treat the Bible just like any other book? Why or why not?
2. Why do you think more Catholics have not taken up the call the study the Scriptures?
3. What, if anything, keeps you from studying the Scriptures more seriously?

Essay Topics and/or Further Study

1. Do more research on the historical critical method. What are the advantages of this research tool? What are the possible disadvantages? Why do you think the Church was cautious about granting permission to use this method?
2. Define other interpretive methodologies, such as textual, historical, literary, source, and redaction methods. What can each one of these methods add to the study of Scripture?
3. Find a Catholic Bible scholar who has lived in the last one hundred years. What are his or her significant contributions? In what way do you see this scholar following the guidelines for Scripture study that the Church has outlined?
4. Choose one of the modern documents on Scripture study to research further: *Divino Afflante Spiritu, Dei Verbum,* or the *Interpretation of Scripture.* Choose one significant passage to summarize and reflect on. How does this document increase your understanding of exegesis?
5. The Youcat explains that the Bible is "like a long letter written by God to each one of us. For this reason I should accept the Sacred Scriptures with great love and reverence." Why is it important to reverence the Bible? In what ways can modern interpretive methods increase our reverence? Are there ways these methods can challenge a biblical scholar's faith? What advice would you give to an aspiring biblical scholar?

Part III: Chapter 2

Criteria for Interpreting Scripture

Memory Verse

> All scripture is inspired by God and profitable for teaching, for reproof, for correction, and for training in righteousness, that the man of God may be complete, equipped for every good work.
>
> —2 Timothy 3:16–17

Key Terms

Catena

Catena Aurea

Historical context

Analogy of Faith

Senses of Scripture

Literal sense

Spiritual sense

Allegorical sense

Typology

Moral sense

Anagogical sense

Questions for Review

1. What is a "catena"?

2. How does historical context help us understand the account of the feeding of the five thousand?

3. What does it mean to read Scripture according to the "Analogy of Faith"?

4. What is the literal sense of Scripture? Give one example.

5. What is the spiritual sense of Scripture? How can it be subdivided? Name and define each.

Quiz

True/False

1. ____ The Church is the proper home for Scripture.
2. ____ Medieval scholars included comments from the Fathers of the Church and other important teachers in the margins of the Bibles they copied.
3. ____ The *Catena Aurea* was assembled by St. Augustine.
4. ____ Knowing the historical context of biblical events helps us to understand their meaning and importance more fully.
5. ____ Reading one passage of Scripture apart from the other books of the Bible gives us enough context to understand its significance.
6. ____ The spiritual sense of Scripture is the meaning conveyed by the words of Scripture.
7. ____ Typology is the study of the connections between the Old and New Testaments.
8. ____ The anagogical sense reveals to us the moral lessons we can draw from Scripture.
9. ____ The allegorical sense of Scripture ties together the events of salvation history.
10 ____ The moral sense of Scripture gives us guidance for our daily lives.

Questions for Discussion

1. Why do you think it's important to listen to what the Fathers and Doctors of the Church have to say about Scripture? What do they have to offer us?
2. Can you think of one truth of the Catholic Faith that helps you understand another truth about the Faith? How do you think not knowing the fullness of the Faith contributes to some people's misunderstandings of it? Can you think of any examples of this?
3. How do you think knowing the different senses of Scripture can enhance your understanding of what you read in the Bible?

Essay Topics and/or Further Study

1. Research further St. Thomas Aquinas's *Cantena Aurea*. Using a free online translation, choose a passage and study what the Church Fathers say. How does the commentary of the Fathers shed light on the different senses of Scripture?
2. Explain all of the senses of Scripture and their meanings. For each "lens" or sense, cite an example from Scripture that illustrates the meaning.
3. Define the Analogy of Faith. Explain, using examples, why it is so important to read Scripture in the context of the Analogy of the Faith.
4. Typology is the study of the connections between the Old and New Testament. Using the *Catechism* and other sources, find an Old Testament "type" that is fulfilled in the New Testament.
5. Look up the readings for this upcoming Sunday Mass. How do all of the readings, studied together, increase your understanding of them? Can you understand the different senses of Scripture of these readings?

Part III: Chapter 3

The Bible in Relation to Science and History

Memory Verse

> In the beginning God created the heavens and the earth. The earth was without form and void, and darkness was upon the face of the deep; and the Spirit of God was moving over the face of the waters.
>
> —Genesis 1:1–2

Key Terms

Fundamentalist interpretation

Textual criticism

Source criticism

"Q"

Qumran

Dead Sea Scrolls

Nag Hammadi

Targumim

Questions for Review

1. How did Pope St. John Paul II describe the relationship of faith and reason?

2. What is a fundamentalist interpretation of the Bible? What does the Church teach about such an interpretation?

3. What is textual criticism?

4. What is source criticism?

5. Name three ancient manuscripts that have been discovered in recent years. How have these helped us better understand the Bible?

Quiz

1. Contrary to a common assumption, ______________________ and the Catholic faith are not incompatible.
2. A __________________ of Scripture does not take historical or literary context into account.
3. ________________________ examines the development of early manuscripts to more accurately establish the earliest form of the Scripture.
4. ______________________ attempts to discern the written and oral origins of an inspired author's writing.
5. "Q" is the nickname of an unknown source of the sayings of ______________ that is now lost.

6. The Dead Sea Scrolls were discovered in 1946 in the caves of ______________.

7. The ________________ are Aramaic paraphrases of the Hebrew Bible.

8. In 1945, a collection of third- and fourth-century Gnostic texts called ________________________ were found in Egypt.

9. We can learn a lot about how the Jewish community in the time of Jesus understood the Scriptures from _________________.

10. Modern scholarship is essential to Catholic ________________.

Questions for Discussion

1. Why do you think so many people believe the Church is anti-science? How can we show people that is not the case?
2. What are the dangers of a fundamentalist interpretation of the Bible? Have you ever witnessed or experienced any of those dangers?
3. Do you ever struggle to believe what you read in the Bible? If so, why? How can some of the different methods and sources discussed in this chapter help you be more confident in your faith?

Essay Topics and/or Further Study

1. In *Divino Afflante Spiritu*, Pope Pius XII writes, "What is the literal sense of a passage is not always as obvious in the speeches and writings of the ancient authors of the East, as it is in the works of our own time." In your own words, what does this mean? Can you find examples in Scripture that illustrate the pope's point? Research those passages to show their deeper meaning. What is the risk of a purely fundamentalist interpretation?
2. Ancient texts like the Dead Sea Scrolls, the Nag Hammadi, and the *targumim* have been discovered in modern times. Choose one of these sources and tell the story of how they were found. What contributions to biblical studies has the source made?
3. Reflect on Pope St. John Paul II's statement that "faith and reason are like two wings on which the human spirit rises to the contemplation of truth." Choose an influential Catholic scientist to research. How did faith and reason factor into their life and work?
4. Recap the four modern methods of criticism used by Scripture scholars: historical, literary, textual, and source criticism. What role does each method play in presenting a fuller understanding of Scripture?
5. Look up the theory of the "Q" source—an important topic in source criticism. What is the evidence for and against "Q"?

Part IV

Overview of the Bible

Part IV: Chapter 1

The Old Testament

Memory Verse

> For whatever was written in former days was written for our instruction, that by steadfastness and the encouragement of the Scriptures we might have hope.
>
> —Romans 15:4

Key Terms

The Old Testament

Covenant

Pentateuch

Torah

Historical books

Prophets

Wisdom literature

Apocryphal

Deuterocanonical

Questions for Review

1. How many books are in the Old Testament?

2. What do covenants form?

3. Whose history does the Old Testament recount?

4. Why do we call the Old Testament "old"?

5. Into what four categories are the various books of the Old Testament divided?

Quiz

1. The Old Testament is made up of ______________ books.
   A. 27
   B. 44
   C. 46

2. The Old Testament tells the history of:
   A. Israel.
   B. Christ.
   C. Abraham.

3. A covenant is a:
   A. formal business arrangement.
   B. legal agreement.
   C. sacred kinship bond.

4. ____________________ is the hinge around which all of history turns.
   A. The Exodus
   B. Jesus
   C. The Old Testament

5. Genesis, Exodus, and Leviticus are books from:
   A. the Pentateuch.
   B. the historical books.
   C. the prophets.

6. Job, Psalms, and Sirach are books from:
   A. the prophets.
   B. the historical books.
   C. the wisdom literature.

7. Joshua, Judges, and Ruth are books from:
   A. the historical books.
   B. the prophets.
   C. the wisdom literature.

8. Lamentations, Hosea, and Nahum are books from:
   A. the prophets.
   B. the wisdom literature.
   C. the historical books.

9. The books Protestants doubt are inspired are labeled:
   A. annotated.
   B. apocryphal.
   C. arbitrary.

10. Deuterocanonical means:
   A. "from Deuteronomy."
   B. "Old Testament canon."
   C. "Second canon."

Questions for Discussion

1. Do you find reading the Old Testament intimidating? Why or why not?
2. Have you ever tried reading the Old Testament from start to finish? If so, how far did you get? Did you stop early? If so, why?
3. Why do you think books that were written so long ago can still speak to people today? Why should they matter to us?

Essay Topics and/or Further Study

1. Define the term "covenant." Contrast a covenant to other forms of legal agreements. Why do you believe God used covenants to establish a relationship with Israel?
2. Research the Pentateuch. What does each book teach us about God's unfolding relationship with Israel?
3. Choose one of the Old Testament prophets to study further. What message did they have for the people of Israel? Is their message relevant for your life today?
4. The wisdom literature is full of some of the most beautifully written poetry in the history of mankind. Nowhere is this more apparent than in the book of Psalms. What is your favorite psalm, and why? Explain why you think this psalm has enduring meaning.
5. *Dei Verbum* says, "God, the inspirer and author of both Testaments, wisely arranged that the New Testament be hidden in the Old and the Old be made manifest in the New." Choose one significant person or event in the Old Testament and demonstrate how there is a New Testament person or event "hidden" in the story. Through this person or event, what was God trying to teach his people?

Part IV: Chapter 2

The New Testament

Memory Verse

> For consider your call, brethren; not many of you were wise according to worldly standards, not many were powerful, not many were of noble birth; but God chose what is foolish in the world to shame the wise, God chose what is weak in the world to shame the strong, God chose what is low and despised in the world, even things that are not, to bring to nothing things that are, so that no human being might boast in the presence of God. He is the source of your life in Christ Jesus, whom God made our wisdom, our righteousness and sanctification and redemption; therefore, as it is written, "Let him who boasts, boast of the Lord."
>
> —1 Corinthians 1:26–31

Key Terms

New Testament

The Gospels

St. Paul

Pauline epistles

Catholic epistles

Questions for Review

1. How many books are in the New Testament?

2. What two histories does the New Testament give us?

3. What are the names of the four Gospel writers?

4. What are the Pauline epistles?

5. What are the Catholic epistles?

Quiz

True/False

1. ____ There are twenty-six books in the New Testament.
2. ____ "Testament" is another word for covenant.
3. ____ The word "gospel" means "proclamation."
4. ____ Acts of the Apostles was written by the Apostle Matthew.
5. ____ St. Paul is the author of both 1 and 2 Corinthians.
6. ____ St. Paul worked as a missionary to the Jews.
7. ____ The Catholic epistles were written for the whole Church.
8. ____ The book of Hebrews explores who the person of Christ is.
9. ____ The book of Revelation is a highly symbolic account of visions by St. Paul.

10 ____ The book of Revelation points to the Second Coming of Christ but does not otherwise shed light on the Catholic faith.

Questions for Discussion

1. Do you find it easier or more difficult to read the New Testament than you do to read the Old?
2. The Church holds that there are no books more important in the whole history of the world than the books of the New Testament. Do you agree or disagree with this statement? Explain.
3. Do you have a favorite book or passage in the New Testament? If so, what is it and why is it your favorite?

Essay Topics and/or Further Study

1. The selected reading from *Dei Verbum* underscores the "preeminence" of New Testament writings. If you were introducing an un-catechized friend to Scripture for the first time, where would you have them begin? Why? What benefits are there to reading the New Testament?
2. Choose one of the Gospel writers to research further. What is unique about his writing style? What seems to be the particular emphasis of his Gospel?
3. There is great value in being able to synthesize the message of a story into a coherent summary. Choose one Gospel to summarize briefly. What are the most important elements of that particular Gospel?
4. Spend some time reading the many writings of St. Paul. From his epistles, what can you discern about his character? Are there any traits you think Catholics should try to emulate?
5. Choose one of the shorter Catholic epistles to study closely. What is the main theme of your chosen letter? What do you think the message meant to the early Christians? Does that same message still have relevance for the Church today?

Part IV: Chapter 3

The Unity of the Old and New Testaments

Memory Verse

> Behold, the days are coming, says the LORD, when I will make a new covenant with the house of Israel and the house of Judah, not like the covenant which I made with their fathers when I took them by the hand to bring them out of the land of Egypt, my covenant which they broke, though I was their husband, says the LORD. But this is the covenant which I will make with the house of Israel after those days, says the LORD: I will put my law within them, and I will write it upon their hearts; and I will be their God, and they shall be my people.
>
> —JEREMIAH 31:31–33

Key Terms

Typology

Covenant

Contract

New Covenant

Questions for Review

1. What is typology and what does it show us?

2. What is one example of an Old Testament "type" concerning the Eucharist?

3. What makes a contract different from a covenant?

4. Who are the five covenant mediators in the Old Testament?

5. Who fulfills all the covenants of the Old Testament?

Quiz

1. St. ______________ wrote, "The New Testament lies hidden in the Old and the Old Testament is unveiled in the New."
   A. Catherine of Siena
   B. Cyril of Alexandria
   C. Augustine

2. People and events from the Old Testament that point to Christ are called:
   A. allegories.
   B. types.
   C. prophecies.

3. Reading the Old Testament in light of the new is called:
   A. exegesis.
   B. soteriology.
   C. typology.

4. A ________________ creates a family bond between two people or groups of people.
   A. contract
   B. covenant
   C. sacrament

5. The ultimate covenant established in salvation history was made by:
   A. Christ.
   B. Abraham.
   C. David.

6. The sign of the covenant with the Israelites was:
   A. the Ten Commandments.
   B. a rainbow.
   C. circumcision.

7. The covenants with Adam and Eve, Noah, Abraham, Moses, and David are collectively called:
   A. salvation history.
   B. the Old Covenant.
   C. Judaism.

8. The sign of the New Covenant is:
   A. the Eucharist.
   B. the cross.
   C. the Magisterium.

9. All of history hinges on:
   A. the birth of the Church at Pentecost.
   B. God's covenant with David.
   C. Jesus.

10. We participate in God's covenant through:
   A. reading Scripture.
   B. the Sacraments.
   C. our hearts.

Questions for Discussion

1. Do you ever struggle to trust God? Why or why not?
2. Typology helps us see the continuity of God's plan for salvation. Do you think that knowing that God has such a carefully executed plan might help you trust him more? Why or why not?
3. How is your life today a participation in salvation history? What connections do you see between you and all the people we've heard about from both the Old and New Testaments?

Essay Topics and/or Further Study

1. Pope Benedict wrote in *Verbum Domini* that "the person of Christ gives unity to all the 'Scriptures' in relation to the one 'Word.'" In what ways does Jesus unify the Scriptures? Think of the high points of the Old Testament. How do they make sense in the light of Christ?
2. Compare contracts and covenants. What is a modern-day example of a contract? What is a modern-day example of a covenant? Which seems to have more value? How do you think covenants are perceived by society?
3. Typology is an incredible method of Scripture study that can give us a deeper understanding of God's plan of salvation. Choose a prominent figure from the Old Testament. How is that figure a "type" of Christ? How does their life or mission help you better understand the role of Jesus?
4. Choose one of the five major covenants from the Old Testament to study further. Who enacts the covenant with God? How is it enacted? What are the signs of the covenant? And did both parties uphold the terms of the covenant? If not, why and how was it broken?
5. The sacraments are the sign of the New Covenant. How does each sacrament change or enhance our covenant relationship with God?

Part V

The Gospels

Part V: Chapter 1

The Gospels' Central Place in Scripture

Memory Verse

> Take my yoke upon you, and learn from me, for I am gentle and lowly in heart, and you will find rest for your souls.
>
> —Matthew 11:29

Key Terms

Gospel

Revelation of God

Incarnate Word

Public revelation

Questions for Review

1. What biblical books stand at the center of Sacred Scripture and salvation history? Why?

2. What does "gospel" mean? Properly speaking, why can we call Jesus "the Gospel"?

3. Why can Jesus tell us about God?

4. Why can Jesus tell us about ourselves?

5. What are the different forms in which the Gospel can be relayed?

Quiz

True/False

1. ____ Jesus Christ stands at the center of salvation history.
2. ____ The Gospels stand at the center of Sacred Scripture.
3. ____ Sacred Scripture is the definitive Revelation of God.
4. ____ Jesus himself can be properly referred to as "the Gospel."
5. ____ Even though Jesus was a man, he was not *fully* man because he was also God.
6. ____ Reading the Gospels can lead us to a personal relationship with God.
7. ____ The history of Revelation can be summarized thus: "In many and various ways God spoke of old to our fathers by the prophets; but in these last days he has spoken to us by a Son."
8. ____ Jesus came to abolish the laws of the prophets and the Old Covenants.
9. ____ Moses was the perfect mediator between God and man.
10. ____ Public revelation was complete by the time of the death of the last apostle.

Questions for Discussion

1. What makes the Good News of Jesus so good?
2. How much do you think about this Good News as you go about your day? What makes it difficult to keep it in mind? What helps you think about it?
3. How often do you share the Good News of Jesus with others? What are some of the ways people have shared it with you that have touched your heart or mind most?

Essay Topics and/or Further Study

1. Write a personal testimony describing when the Gospel became meaningful for you in a deep way. Is there a time when the Good News of Jesus "clicked" with you, perhaps during a reading in Mass or on your own?
2. The Gospel can be related through preaching, the liturgy, and scriptural writings. What are the advantages of encountering the Gospel in each of these forms?
3. In the selected reading, we read that "Saint John marveled at this inexhaustible mystery that touches even our senses. He recalled that Jesus was 'heard . . . seen . . . looked upon . . . touched . . . and was made manifest to us' (1 John 1:1–2). With this in mind, find an account in the Gospels of someone who had a personal interaction with Jesus. Writing in first person, describe what that person experienced, and use sensorial language to describe the account. What did this person see, and what did Jesus see in them? What was it like to speak with, listen to, and touch the Son of God?
4. Using the discussion questions from this chapter, interview a Christian who is older than you. How do their responses about the Gospel relate or differ to your own?
5. Research and tell the story of a saint who was particularly moved or experienced a conversion when they were first exposed to the Gospel.

Part V: Chapter 2

The Synoptic Gospels: Matthew, Mark, and Luke

Memory Verse

> When the Spirit of truth comes, he will guide you into all the truth; for he will not speak on his own authority, but whatever he hears he will speak, and he will declare to you the things that are to come.

—John 16:13

Key Terms

Synoptic

Infancy narrative

Parables

Miracles

Paschal mystery

Synoptic problem

Questions for Review

1. What are the three Synoptic Gospels?

2. What is the advantage of having three Gospels that are so similar?

3. How should we understand the seeming contradictions in the Synoptic Gospels?

4. What purpose do the miracles in the Synoptic Gospels serve?

5. What is the paschal mystery?

Quiz

1. The main focus of Matthew's Gospel is how Jesus brings ________________ into the world.
2. The main focus of Mark's Gospel is to gradually reveal Jesus's ____________.
3. St. Luke's Gospel emphasizes that while salvation is from the Jews, Jesus extends to embrace ________________.
4. ________________ means "seeing the whole together."
5. Scripture scholars refer to the Christmas story as the __________________.
6. The Gospels are completely accurate in the sense that they always convey the ___________ of what happened.

7. ______________, similar to short stories, convey complex truths in a simple and easy to understand form.

8. ______________ were one way for Jesus to reveal the kingdom of God.

9. The climax of the Gospels is the ____________________.

10. Questions surrounding the similarities of the Synoptic Gospels and their relationship to one another is referred to as ____________________________.

Questions for Discussion

1. Have you ever read or heard three similar but slightly different accounts of an event: a game, a show, a fight, etc.? Why were the accounts different? How did those differences help you better understand what happened?
2. Have you ever been like the prodigal son—needing forgiveness, but afraid to ask? How does this parable help you understand the love of God the Father?
3. When you read the Synoptic Gospels, what impression do they give you of Jesus and his ministry? What strikes you the most about Jesus as he is depicted in these Gospels?

Essay Topics and/or Further Study

1. The Pontifical Biblical Commission's document "Historical Truth of the Gospels" sheds light on how the Gospels were formed over a period of time in three stages: the life and teaching of Jesus, the oral tradition, and the written tradition. What points does the commission make about each of the stages? In what ways do the three stages lend to the credibility of the Gospel? How would you respond to criticism saying that the process, like a game of telephone, might leave out important information?
2. Each of the Synoptic Gospels has a particular style that reflects its author's sensibilities. Choose one of the Synoptic Gospels to read in full, and then write a review of that Gospel. What is important to the author? How would you describe them as a storyteller? Research the Gospel writer as well. How does their background influence their writing?
3. Using a good study Bible, examine closely one of the parables of Jesus from the Synoptic Gospels. Retell the parable in your own words, using the study Bible to help you underline Jesus's message. Now discuss what the parable means in the life of a Christian.

4. The practice of *lectio divina* encourages us to put ourselves into the stories of Scripture, using our imagination, to better contemplate what it would be like to be present for the events of the Bible. Retell one of Jesus's miracles from a first-person perspective. Describe not only the surroundings but your feelings about the situation.

5. Re-read about the temptation of Jesus in Matthew 4:1–11, Mark 1:12–13, and Luke 4:1–13. Find the Old Testament verses that Jesus quotes. With the help of an online Scripture commentary, explain the significance of each verse and why, in the context of Satan's offer, it has significance not only for Jesus but for all Christians.

Part V: Chapter 3

The Gospel of John

Memory Verse

> There was a man sent from God, whose name was John. He came for testimony, to bear witness to the light, that all might believe through him. He was not the light, but came to bear witness to the light.
>
> —John 1:6–8

Key Terms

John

Logos

Signs

High Christology

Questions for Review

1. What are the seven signs in John's Gospel?

2. What are the seven "I AM" statements?

3. Why is the number seven significant?

4. In what chapter of his Gospel does John present Jesus's teaching on the Eucharist?

5. How does John's account of the Last Supper differ from the Synoptic Gospels' account?

Quiz

True/False

1. ____ John's Gospel is primarily written for Gentiles.
2. ____ John's Gospel combines biographical facts with prayer insight.
3. ____ The Gospel of John shows that Jesus is at the center of creation.
4. ____ John frequently refers to Jesus as "the Word."
5. ____ To illustrate who Jesus is, John gives us seven parables worked by Jesus.
6. ____ Seven is the biblical number of completion.
7. ____ "I AM" was the name God gave himself in the Old Testament.
8. ____ Many scholars believe that John's Gospel presents a "high Christology," which means he focuses on Jesus's humanity.
9. ____ In Jesus's "High Priestly Prayer," he institutes the Eucharist.
10. ____ John was a firsthand witness to the Crucifixion.

Questions for Discussion

1. What do you think is the advantage of having John's Gospel, which is different in so many ways from the Synoptic Gospels?
2. What do you know about Jesus from John's Gospel that you wouldn't know otherwise about him? Why does this matter?
3. What does it mean to you to be a "beloved disciple?" Do you see yourself this way? Why or why not?

Essay Topics and/or Further Study

1. St. John's Gospel is not uncommonly referred to as an exquisite piece of literature. Describe St. John's writing style. In what ways do you think his literature style makes the Gospel valuable?
2. Reflect on Pope Benedict XVI's General Audience on St. John the Apostle. Using points from his talk, explain what unique perspective St. John's Gospel provides for the Church.
3. Study the seven "signs" of Jesus in John's Gospel. Summarize each. Do they have any common features? Taken as a whole, what do they tell us about Jesus and his mission?
4. The Gospel of John features a "high Christology," meaning he focuses on Jesus's divinity. In what ways can you see the divinity of Christ reflected through John's Gospel?
5. St. John refers to himself as "the beloved Disciple." Put yourself in his place as a dear friend of Jesus. What would your conversations be like? Would you have the courage to rest your head on the shoulder of God's Son? Why do you think it is important to recognize that Jesus valued intimate human friendship?

Final Exam ______ / 100

Matching

2 points each

A. Anthropology
B. The Fall
C. Natural Revelation
D. Divine Revelation
E. St. Thomas Aquinas
F. Relativism
G. Scholasticism
H. St. John the Baptist
I. The Magisterium
J. *Theopneustos*
K. Inerrancy
L. Apocryphal
M. Gnosticism
N. Theology
O. *lectio divina*
P. Exegesis
Q. Typology
R. Covenant
S. Gospel
T. Pascal Mystery
U. Greek
V. St. John
W. 27
X. 46
Y. Deuterocanonical

_____ 1. Forms sacred kinship/family bonds
_____ 2. Came up with five proofs for God
_____ 3. The belief that Scripture is "free from all error"
_____ 4. The task of interpreting Scripture
_____ 5. Refers to the passion, death, resurrection, and ascension of Jesus
_____ 6. The study or understanding of the human person
_____ 7. Not authentic; term given to books the Protestants removed from the Catholic Bible
_____ 8. Means "good news"
_____ 9. The study of the connections between the Old and New Testaments
_____ 10. Denies the humanity of Christ
_____ 11. The study of God
_____ 12. Method of engaging with Scripture through reading, meditation, prayer, and contemplation
_____ 13. Means "God-breathed"
_____ 14. Prophet that helps bridge the Old and New Testaments
_____ 15. The first time humans sinned
_____ 16. How God reveals himself directly to humanity
_____ 17. His Gospel is not one of the Synoptic Gospels
_____ 18. How God reveals himself through creation
_____ 19. The claim that truth does not exist
_____ 20. Means "second canon"
_____ 21. The movement to integrate philosophical method and Christianity
_____ 22. The authoritative office in the Church that interprets Scripture and preserves the Deposit of Faith
_____ 23. The New Testament's first language
_____ 24. This many books are in the Old Testament
_____ 25. This many books are in the New Testament

Short Answer

5 points each

1. What is dynamic equivalency?

2. What is textual criticism?

3. What is source criticism?

4. In what two ways is Divine Revelation transmitted to each new generation? Define each way.

5. Name the four groups of mysteries we meditate on while praying the Rosary.

6. What is meant by the phrase “the canon of Scripture”?

7. Who did God use to mediate his five Old Testament covenants?

8. Which three Gospels are considered the Synoptic Gospels?

9. What is the literal sense of Scripture? Give one example.

10. What is the spiritual sense of Scripture? How can it be subdivided? Name and define each.

Answer Key

Part I: Chapter 1 – The Desire for God

Questions for Review

1. What does "anthropology" mean?

Anthropology is the study or understanding of the human person.

2. What does it mean to be created in God's image?

It means that man was created with both a physical body and a spiritual soul, with the capacity to reason, choose right from wrong, and make a gift of himself in love.

3. What is the "Fall"?

The Fall is a term given to the first time humans sinned, when Adam and Eve ate of the forbidden fruit.

4. When man and woman sinned, what did they lose?

When man and woman sinned, they lost friendship with God.

5. What problems have we inherited from our first parents?

From our first parents we have inherited original sin: a wounded relationship with God and a tendency to hide from God.

Quiz

1. B
2. False
3. C
4. A
5. B
6. C
7. C
8. B
9. C
10. A

Part I: Chapter 2 – Natural Revelation

Questions for Review

1. What is Natural Revelation?

Natural Revelation is how God reveals himself to humanity through the created order.

2. What is looking at God's creation supposed to lead us to do?

Looking at God's creation should lead us to glorify the Creator.

3. Can we know that God exists by reason alone?

Yes, we can know that God exists by reason alone, by studying the physical world.

4. Name and explain each of St. Thomas Aquinas's five ways for knowing God from Natural Revelation.

    1. **Argument from Motion: "Whatever is in motion is put in motion by another." At some point in the universe's history, there must be a first (or "prime") mover. The mover is God.**
    2. **Argument from Causation: The existence of everything has been passed on through a series of causes and effects. Trace the series of causes and effects in the world back to the moment of nothingness. Nothing can cause itself. There must be a first (or uncaused) cause. This cause is God.**
    3. **Argument from Contingency: Everything that exists has the real potential for non-existence. There must be an absolutely necessary being not contingent upon anything else, but upon whom everything else depends. This necessary being is God.**
    4. **Argument from Degrees of Perfection: Persons and things have various degrees of perfections, such as goodness, beauty, truth, etc. No single created person or thing possesses all perfection. There must be a being who possesses all perfection and whose perfection is the standard by which we measure everything else. This being who is the standard of all goodness, perfection, and truth is God.**
    5. **Argument from Design: There are systems in the universe so intricate and perfect that they demonstrate a supreme intelligence as their cause. This intelligence cannot be accounted for by any intelligence we know. It is reasonable to conclude that there exists a supremely intelligent and powerful being who is the author of all that exists. This author is God.**

5. What is relativism? How does it undermine reason?

Relativism is the claim that truth does not exist. Relativism directly undermines reason, which affirms that humanity is capable of ascertaining real truth about God.

Quiz

1. The created world/nature/creation
2. Scholasticism
3. put in motion by another/something else
4. Cause
5. Degrees of Perfection
6. Supremely intelligent being
7. The Enlightenment
8. Relativism
9. soul
10. to know and be with God

Part 1: Chapter 3 – Divine Revelation

Questions for Review

1. Who are the Patriarchs? What is their relationship to one another and to God?

Abraham, Isaac, and Jacob are the Patriarchs, or fathers of the people of Israel. Abraham is the father of Isaac, and Isaac is the father of Jacob. God made a covenant with Abraham, promising that he would become the father of many nations. This covenant with God was passed on to both Isaac and Jacob.

2. Through whom did God give the Law to Israel, and under whom did God establish Israel as a great kingdom?

God gave the Law to Israel through Moses. Under David, God established Israel as a great kingdom.

3. Which prophet bridged the gap between the Old Testament and the New?

John the Baptist bridged the gap between the Old Testament and the New.

4. Who is the summation of the Scriptures and why?

Jesus Christ is the summation of all the Scriptures because all of Scripture "speaks of Christ and finds its fulfilment in Christ."

5. In what two ways is Divine Revelation transmitted to each new generation? Define each way.

Divine Revelation is transmitted to each new generation through Sacred Scripture and Sacred Tradition. Sacred Scripture is the preaching of the apostles, or "oral tradition," written down and preserved as the New Testament of the Bible. Sacred Tradition is the living transmission of Divine Revelation in the doctrine, life, and worship of the Church.

Quiz

True/False

1. True
2. False: Leviticus
3. True
4. False: Numbers is not a book of Wisdom Literature
5. True
6. False: The Deposit of Faith
7. True
8. False: the Magisterium
9. False: They must be active in their faith and participate in many spheres of influence: social, economic, political, etc.
10. True

Part II: Chapter 1 – Divine Inspiration

Questions for Review

1. Who inspired the Sacred Scriptures?

The Holy Spirit inspired the human authors to write the Sacred Scriptures.

2. What does it mean to take historical context into account when studying the Scriptures?

We take historical context into account when studying the Scriptures by considering the time and place—the historical, political, social, and cultural contexts—in which the biblical books were written to better understand the authors' meaning.

3. What does it mean to take literary context into account when studying the Scriptures?

We take literary context into account when studying the Scriptures by considering the literary form of the passage we are reading. Understanding the type of text—history, poetry, parables, prophecies, and other literary forms—helps us interpret the authors' meaning more accurately.

4. What is inerrancy?

Inerrancy is the belief that Scripture is "free from all error." It means that everything written in the Bible is supposed to be there as part of God's plan for our salvation.

5. Is everything in the Bible "literally" true? Explain.

Not everything in the Bible is *literally* true. We must take into consideration historical context, literary form, and the guidance of the Church's Magisterium.

Quiz

1. human authors / the Holy Spirit
2. Divine Inspiration
3. "God-breathed"
4. The Bible/Sacred Scripture
5. historical context
6. historical and/or literary context; intention/meaning
7. Literary context
8. Inerrant / error
9. St. Augustine
10. Magisterium

Part II: Chapter 2 – How Was the Bible Put Together?

Questions for Review

1. What is Oral Tradition?

The preaching of the Gospel by the apostles is referred to as Oral Tradition.

2. What do we mean by the phrase "the canon of Scripture"?

The canon of Scripture refers to the forty-six books in the Old Testament and the twenty-seven books in the New Testament that the Catholic Church accepts as inspired.

3. For the early Church, what was the ultimate criteria for a book being granted canonical status?

The ultimate criterion for canonical status in the early Church was that a book was accepted as Scripture in the apostolic tradition of the Church.

4. By what century did the bishops first give us the canon of Scripture that the Church still uses today?

In the fourth century, Pope St. Damasus and the bishops assembled at the Synod of Rome in 382 promulgated a list of canonical books the Church still holds today.

5. What is dynamic equivalency?

Dynamic equivalency differs from a literal translation, which translates the text word for word. Instead, dynamic equivalency uses different words or different figures of speech in the attempt to preserve the actual, deeper meaning of the original.

Quiz

1. A
2. B
3. C
4. A
5. A
6. C
7. B
8. A
9. C
10. B

Part II: Chapter 3 – Sacred Scripture in the Life of the Church

Questions for Review

1. What is theology?

Theology is the study of God.

2. What is another name for the Liturgy of the Hours? What is the role of Scripture in this prayer?

Another name for the Liturgy of the Hours is the Divine Office. The Hours of the Divine Office integrate the singing of the Psalms with other readings from Scripture, as well as prayers, hymns, and readings from the Fathers and Doctors of the Church.

3. Name three prayers in the Mass that are drawn from Sacred Scripture.

Our prayer before communion: "Lord I am not worthy that you would enter under my roof, but only say the word and my soul shall be healed" (Mt 8:8).

The Gloria

Eucharistic prayers

Other possible answers: The Penitential Act, The Preparation of the Altar, The Hosanna (Preface Acclamation), The Lord's Prayer.

4. What is *lectio divina*?

***Lectio divina* is a prayerful method of reading Scripture through four steps: reading, meditation, prayer, and contemplation.**

5. How does the Rosary incorporate Scripture into personal prayer?

The main prayers of the Rosary are themselves scriptural (the Our Father and Hail Mary). The Rosary invites us to meditate on twenty mysteries in the life of Jesus and his mother. Most of these mysteries are recorded in Scripture.

Quiz

True/False

1. True
2. False; seven
3. False; Jewish temple worship
4. False; ambo
5. True
6. False; the Mass
7. True
8. True
9. False; The Assumption and Coronation of Mary are prefigured in Scripture but are drawn from Sacred Tradition, not recorded directly in Scripture as events
10. True

Part III: Chapter 1 – Authentic Interpretation of Scripture

Question for Review

1. What is exegesis?

The task of interpreting Scripture is called exegesis.

2. What are the goals of the historical-critical method?

The goals of the historical-critical method are to use research techniques to better understand past events, learn more about the writers of certain texts, and discern fact from fiction in historical narratives.

3. How did *Divino Afflante Spiritu* affect biblical scholarship?

***Divino Afflante Spiritu* opened the door to wider use of historical methods of biblical interpretation and encouraged the use of the original languages of Scriptures (Hebrew and Greek) for study and translation.**

4. What was the Second Vatican Council's document on Sacred Scripture called?

The Second Vatican Council's document on Sacred Scripture was called *Dei Verbum*.

5. What is a common theme of all the modern Church documents on Scripture?

The common theme of all the modern Church documents on Scripture is an encouragement for Catholics to study the Scriptures.

Quiz

1. B
2. C
3. B
4. C
5. A
6. B
7. C
8. A
9. A
10. B

Part III: Chapter 2 – Criteria for Interpreting Scripture

Questions for Review

1. What is a "catena"?

A "catena," which in Latin means "chain," is a compilation of important comments on Scripture published together into a chain of commentary within the very text of the Bible.

2. How does historical context help us understand the account of the feeding of the five thousand?

Historical context helps us understand many things about the feeding of the five thousand. Understanding the value of "two hundred denarii" in John 6:7 helps us understand how large the crowd was and how expensive it would be to feed them. Understanding that the barley loaves mentioned in John 6:9 were eaten mostly by the poor shows us that Jesus based his miracle on the generosity of a poor boy. Understanding that the Jews at the time hoped their messiah would be a military leader helps us understand why, in John 6:15, though the Jews wanted to make Jesus king, he could not allow it.

3. What does it mean to read Scripture according to the "Analogy of Faith"?

To read Scripture according to the Analogy of Faith means to relate it to the totality of Scripture and Tradition (piecing together and "linking" all the aspects of our Catholic Faith).

4. What is the literal sense of Scripture? Give one example.

The literal sense of Scripture is the meaning that comes directly from the text and is intended by the inspired author. The *Catechism* defines it as the "meaning conveyed by the words of Scripture and discovered by exegesis, following the rules of sound interpretation" (CCC 116). One example is the feeding of the five thousand in John 6:1–15: the literal sense is the story itself.

5. What is the spiritual sense of Scripture? How can it be subdivided? Name and define each.

The spiritual sense of Scripture is the deeper meaning that reveals something about God's plan. It can be subdivided into the allegorical sense (which shows how people and events in the Old Testament prefigure the fulfillment of God's plan in Christ), the moral sense (which shows us the moral lessons we can draw from the stories of Scripture), and the anagogical sense (which helps us to view the events of Scripture in light of their eternal significance).

Quiz

True/False

1. True
2. True
3. False; St. Thomas Aquinas
4. True
5. False; Reading one passage in the context of all Scripture and Tradition, according to the Analogy of Faith, gives us the proper insights.
6. False; the literal sense
7. True
8. False; the moral sense
9. True
10. True

Part III: Chapter 3 – The Bible in Relation to Science and History

Questions for Review

1. How did Pope St. John Paul II describe the relationship of faith and reason?

Pope St. John Paul II said that "faith and reason are like two wings on which the human spirit rises to the contemplation of truth."

2. What is a fundamentalist interpretation of the Bible? What does the Church teach about such an interpretation?

A fundamentalist interpretation is one that insists on a "literal" interpretation that fails to account for historical context and leads to conflict with the findings of modern science. The Church rejects this type of interpretation, because a proper understanding of Scripture takes into account the historical circumstances of the author and the different forms of writing used in that time.

3. What is textual criticism?

Textual criticism is a method of examining the development of early manuscripts (which were copied by hand and thus were prone to minor mistakes) to more accurately establish the earliest form of the text.

4. What is source criticism?

Source criticism attempts to determine what written and oral sources the inspired authors drew from.

5. Name three ancient manuscripts that have been discovered in recent years. How have these helped us better understand the Bible?

Three ancient manuscripts discovered in recent years are the Dead Sea Scrolls (which include the earliest copies of many parts of the Old Testament, which are crucial to source criticism), the Nag Hammadi (which gives us insight into the Gnostic heresy), and the *targumim* (which helps us understand how the Jews around the time of Jesus understood the Scriptures and are important for textual criticism of the Old Testament).

Quiz

1. Science
2. fundamentalist interpretation
3. Textual criticism
4. Source criticism
5. Jesus
6. Qumran
7. *targumim*
8. the Nag Hammadi
9. the *targumim*
10. exegesis

Part IV: Chapter 1 – The Old Testament

Questions for Review

1. How many books are in the Old Testament?

There are forty-six books in the Old Testament.

2. What do covenants form?

Covenants form sacred kinship bonds that make families.

3. Whose history does the Old Testament recount?

The Old Testament recounts the history of the Israelites, which is the history of the family of Christ, the Church.

4. Why do we call the Old Testament "old"?

We call the Old Testament "old" because it recounts events that took place long before Jesus's birth (and so it is actually "old") and because it tells the story of the covenants God made with mankind that were fulfilled with the coming of Christ and his establishment of a "New Testament" or "Covenant."

5. Into what four categories are the various books of the Old Testament divided?

The Old Testament books are divided into the Pentateuch (or Torah), the historical books, the prophets, and wisdom literature.

Quiz

1. C
2. A
3. C
4. B
5. A
6. C
7. A
8. A
9. B
10. C

Part IV: Chapter 2 – The New Testament

Questions for Review

1. How many books are in the New Testament?

There are twenty-seven books in the New Testament.

2. What two histories does the New Testament give us?

The New Testament gives us the history of the Incarnation and the history of the Church.

3. What are the names of the four Gospel writers?

The four Gospel writers are Matthew, Mark, Luke, and John.

4. What are the Pauline epistles?

The Pauline epistles are the letters written by St. Paul to communities of Christians.

5. What are the Catholic epistles?

The Catholic ("universal") letters are letters that were written to the entire Church rather than to a particular community.

Quiz

True/False

1. False: 27
2. True
3. False: "good news"
4. False: St. Luke the Evangelist
5. True
6. False: to the Gentiles
7. True
8. True
9. False: St. John
10. False: it sheds light on many teachings, such as the Mass and heaven

Part IV: Chapter 3 – The Unity of the Old and New Testaments

Questions for Review

1. What is typology and what does it show us?

Typology is reading the Old Testament and New Testament in light of the other and seeing how events, people, places, and things from one Testament point to or are illuminated by the other. It shows us the unity of the Old and New Testaments.

2. What is one example of an Old Testament "type" concerning the Eucharist?

One example of an Old Testament "type" for the Eucharist is the Passover. It prefigures Christ's sacrifice on the cross and the Eucharist. (Another type of the Eucharist is the manna the Israelites ate in the desert).

3. What makes a contract different from a covenant?

In a contract, goods or services are exchanged under narrow conditions. In a covenant, a person exchanges *themselves* in order to be united to another in an intimate way.

4. Who are the five covenant mediators in the Old Testament?

The five covenant mediators in the Old Testament are Adam and Eve, Noah and his family, Abraham and his descendants, Moses and the Israelites, and David and the Kingdom of Israel.

5. Who fulfills all the covenants of the Old Testament?

All of the covenants of the Old Testament are fulfilled through Jesus Christ.

Quiz

1. C
2. B
3. C
4. B
5. A
6. A
7. B
8. A
9. C
10. B

Part V: Chapter 1 – The Gospels' Central Place in Scripture

Questions for Review

1. What biblical books stand at the center of Sacred Scripture and salvation history? Why?

The Gospels are at the center of Sacred Scripture and salvation history because through them we encounter God telling us about himself.

2. What does "gospel" mean? Properly speaking, why can we call Jesus "the Gospel"?

"Gospel" means "Good News." We can properly call Jesus "the Gospel" because he is the "Good News" and the Word of God.

3. Why can Jesus tell us about God?

Jesus can tell us about God because he is God.

4. Why can Jesus tell us about ourselves?

Jesus can tell us about ourselves because, since he was also a man, he reveals mankind perfectly to us as well.

5. What are the different forms in which the Gospel can be relayed?

The Gospel can be relayed through preaching, the liturgy, and scriptural writings.

Quiz

True/False

1. True
2. True
3. False: Jesus
4. True
5. False: he was both fully man and fully God
6. True
7. True
8. False: he came to fulfil them
9. False: Jesus
10. True

Part V: Chapter 2 – The Synoptic Gospels: Matthew, Mark, and Luke

Questions for Review

1. What are the three Synoptic Gospels?

The three Synoptic Gospels are Matthew, Mark, and Luke.

2. What is the advantage of having three Gospels that are so similar?

The advantage of having three Gospels that are so similar is that we learn more by having multiple accounts of the same event than if we only had one.

3. How should we understand the seeming contradictions in the Synoptic Gospels?

Where there are seeming contradictions in the Synoptic Gospels, we should look to what truth is being conveyed and find the meaning of the event that harmonizes the differences in the different accounts.

4. What purpose do the miracles in the Synoptic Gospels serve?

In the Synoptic Gospels, Jesus's miracles not only witness to his divine power, but also reveal the kingdom of God coming into the world and healing its brokenness.

5. What is the paschal mystery?

The paschal mystery are the events of Jesus's passion, death, resurrection, and ascension.

Quiz

1. the Kingdom/the Kingdom of God
2. identity
3. the whole world/the lowly/the broken/the outcast
4. synoptic
5. "Infancy Narrative"
6. truth
7. Parables
8. Miracles
9. Paschal Mystery
10. the Synoptic Problem

Part V: Chapter 3 – The Gospel of John

Questions for Review

1. What are the seven signs in John's Gospel?

The seven signs in John's Gospel are (1) the miracle at Cana, (2) the healing of the official's son, (3) the healing of the paralytic, (4) the multiplication of the loaves, (5) the restoration of the blind man, (6) the raising of Lazarus, and (7) the resurrection of Jesus.

2. What are the seven "I AM" statements?

The seven "I AM" statements are: (1) I am the bread of life, (2) I am the light of the world, (3) I am the door of the sheep, (4) I am the good shepherd, (5) I am the resurrection and the life, (6) I am the way, the truth, and the life, and (7) I am the true vine.

3. Why is the number seven significant?

The number seven is significant because it points back to the seven days of creation in Genesis 1, and because it is the number of completion.

4. In what chapter of his Gospel does John present Jesus's teaching on the Eucharist?

The presentation of Jesus's teaching on the Eucharist is found in John 6.

5. How does John's account of the Last Supper differ from the Synoptic Gospels' account?

John's account of the Last Supper differs from the Synoptic Gospels' account in that it does not provide the institution narrative concerning the Eucharist but instead relates Jesus's teachings and prayers of that night over four chapters.

Quiz

True/False

1. False: Jewish Christians
2. True
3. True
4. True
5. False: seven "signs" or miracles
6. True
7. True
8. False: focuses on his divinity
9. False: he passes his mission on to the apostles
10. True

Final Exam

Matching

2 points each

1. R
2. E
3. K
4. P
5. T
6. A
7. L
8. S
9. Q
10. M
11. N
12. O
13. J
14. H
15. B
16. D
17. V
18. C
19. F
20. Y
21. G
22. I
23. U
24. X
25. W

Short Answer

5 points each

1. What is dynamic equivalency?

Dynamic equivalency is a technique used in translating Scripture. It differs from a literal translation, which translates the text word for word, and instead seeks to find the underlying meaning of a given passage. It uses different words or different figures of speech in the attempt to preserve the actual, deeper meaning of the original.

2. What is textual criticism?

Textual criticism is a method of examining the development of early manuscripts (which were copied by hand and thus were prone to minor mistakes) to more accurately establish the earliest form of the text.

3. What is source criticism?

Source criticism attempts to determine what written and oral sources the inspired authors drew from.

4. In what two ways is Divine Revelation transmitted to each new generation? Define each way.

Divine Revelation is transmitted to each new generation through Sacred Scripture and Sacred Tradition. Sacred Scripture is the preaching of the apostles, or "oral tradition," written down and preserved as the New Testament of the Bible. Sacred Tradition is the living transmission of Divine Revelation in the doctrine, life, and worship of the Church.

5. Name the four groups of mysteries we meditate on while praying the Rosary.

Joyful, Sorrowful, Luminous, and Glorious

6. What is meant by the phrase "the canon of Scripture"?

The canon of Scripture refers to the forty-six books in the Old Testament and the twenty-seven books in the New Testament that the Catholic Church accepts as inspired.

7. Who did God use to mediate his five Old Testament covenants?

Adam and Eve, Noah, Abraham, Moses, and David

8. Which three Gospels are considered the Synoptic Gospels?

Mark, Matthew, and Luke

9. What is the literal sense of Scripture? Give one example.

The literal sense of Scripture is the meaning that comes directly from the text and is intended by the inspired author. The *Catechism* defines it as the "meaning conveyed by the words of Scripture and discovered by exegesis, following the rules of sound interpretation" (CCC 116). One example is the feeding of the five thousand in John 6:1–15: the literal sense is the story itself.

10. What is the spiritual sense of Scripture? How can it be subdivided? Name and define each.

The spiritual sense of Scripture is the deeper meaning that reveals something about God's plan. It can be subdivided into the allegorical sense (which shows how people and events in the Old Testament prefigure the fulfillment of God's plan in Christ), the moral sense (which shows us the moral lessons we can draw from the stories of Scripture), and the anagogical sense (which helps us to view the events of Scripture in light of their eternal significance).